CPS-Morrill ES

3245712100016 4

Edison, Erin   SP 551.5 EDI
Luz del sol

W9-BEC-786

DATE DUE

SP   BC#32457121000164 $18.49
551.5   Edison, Erin
EDI   Luz del sol

Morrill ES
Chicago Public Schools
6011 S. Rockwell St.
Chicago, IL 60629

Luz del sol
Sunlight

Lo básico sobre el tiempo
Weather Basics

por/by Erin Edison

Editora consultora/Consulting Editor:

Gail Saunders-Smith, PhD

CAPSTONE PRESS
a capstone imprint

Pebble Plus is published by Capstone Press,
1710 Roe Crest Drive, North Mankato, Minnesota 56003
www.capstonepub.com

Copyright © 2013 by Capstone Press, a Capstone imprint. All rights reserved. No part of this publication may
be reproduced in whole or in part, or stored in a retrieval system, or transmitted in any form or by any means,
electronic, mechanical, photocopying, recording, or otherwise, without written permission of the publisher.

Library of Congress Cataloging-in-Publication Data
Edison, Erin.
  [Sunlight. Spanish & English]
  Luz del sol = Sunlight / por Erin Edison ; Gail Saunders-Smith, Editora consultora.
     p. cm.—(Pebble plus bilingüe. Lo básico sobre el tiempo = Pebble plus bilingual. Weather basics)
  Includes index.
  ISBN 978-1-62065-166-7 (library binding)
  ISBN: 978-1-4765-1768-1 (ebook PDF)
1. Sunshine—Juvenile literature. 2. Sun—Temperature—Juvenile literature. I. Saunders-Smith, Gail. II. Title. III. Title:
Sunlight.
QC911.2.E3518 2013
551.5'271—dc23   2012017695

Summary: Simple text and full-color photographs describe sunlight and how it causes temperature changes, the seasons,
wind, and clouds—in both English and Spanish

Editorial Credits
Erika L. Shores, editor; Strictly Spanish, translation services; Kyle Grenz, designer; Eric Manske, bilingual book
designer; Laura Manthe, production specialist

Photo Credits
Alamy: PSL Images/NASA, 11, PVstock.com, 7; Dreamstime: Afhunta, 15, Alexstar, 12, 14, Optimist79, 21,
Pozn, back cover; Getty Images Inc.: Taxi/Barbara Peacock, 17; PhotoEdit Inc.: James Shaffer, 19; Shutterstock:
Andriano, cover, djgis, 1, Efired, 9, Peter Sobolev, 13, Vibrant Image Studio, 5

Artistic Effects
Shutterstock: marcus55

**Capstone Press thanks Mike Shores, earth science teacher at RBA Public Charter School in Mankato,
Minnesota, for his assistance on this book.**

Note to Parents and Teachers

The Lo básico sobre el tiempo/Weather Basics series supports national science standards related
to earth science. This book describes and illustrates sunlight. The images support early readers
in understanding the text. The repetition of words and phrases helps early readers learn new
words. This book also introduces early readers to subject-specific vocabulary words, which are
defined in the Glossary section. Early readers may need assistance to read some words and to
use the Table of Contents, Glossary, Internet Sites, and Index sections of the book.

Printed in China.
092012   006934LEOS13

Table of Contents

Tabla de contenidos

Sunlight

Sunlight comes right

from the sun.

It gives Earth light and heat.

It makes Earth's weather.

Luz del sol

La luz del sol viene

directamente del Sol.

Le da a la Tierra luz y calor.

Forma el tiempo de la Tierra.

Sunlight travels in rays.
The rays heat Earth's atmosphere
unevenly. It causes pockets of cool
and warm air. These air pockets
move and cause wind.

La luz del sol viaja en rayos.
Los rayos calientan la atmósfera
de la Tierra en forma despareja.
Esto causa pozos de aire fríos y calientes.
Estos pozos de aire se mueven y
causan viento.

Sunlight heats bodies of water.

The heat causes water

to evaporate into the air.

Clouds form and carry water around Earth.

La luz del sol calienta los cuerpos de agua.

El calor causa que el agua se

evapore en el aire.

Las nubes se forman y llevan agua

alrededor de la Tierra.

Day and Night

The sun lights half of Earth at a time.

When it's day on one side,

it's night on the other.

As Earth spins, places move

in and out of light.

Día y noche

El Sol ilumina la mitad de la Tierra a la vez.

Cuando es de día en un lado, es noche del otro.

Mientras la Tierra gira, los lugares se mueven

dentro y fuera de la luz.

Sun and Earth

Sunlight is strongest at places near the equator. The sun shines directly down on this area.
All the sunlight makes the air hot.

El Sol y la Tierra

La luz del sol es más fuerte en lugares cerca del ecuador. El Sol brilla directamente sobre esta área. Toda la luz del sol hace que el aire se caliente.

equator/
ecuador

13

The sun's rays hit Earth's poles at an angle.
The weak sunlight doesn't
warm the air as much.
Ice and snow cover the poles all year.

Los rayos del sol golpean los polos de la Tierra en ángulo. La luz del sol débil no calienta mucho el aire. El hielo y la nieve cubren los polos todo el año.

North Pole/ Polo Norte

South Pole / Polo Sur

15

In June, Earth's top half

is tilted toward the sun.

It's summer here.

Earth's bottom half gets less sun.

It's winter there.

En junio, la mitad superior de la Tierra

está inclinada hacia el Sol.

Es verano aquí.

La mitad inferior de la Tierra recibe menos sol.

Es invierno ahí.

In December, the top of Earth is

tilted away from the sun.

It's winter here.

More sunlight hits the bottom half of Earth.

It's summer there.

En diciembre, la mitad superior de la Tierra está

inclinada alejada del Sol.

Es invierno aquí.

Más luz del sol llega a la mitad inferior de la Tierra.

Es verano ahí.

We Need the Sun

Plants wouldn't grow without sunlight.

Animals wouldn't have food.

Without the sun's heat, oceans would freeze.

Sunlight makes life on Earth possible.

Necesitamos el Sol

Las plantas no crecerían sin luz del sol.

Los animales no tendrían alimentos.

Sin el calor del sol, los océanos se congelarían.

La luz del sol hace posible la vida en la Tierra.

21

Glossary

atmosphere—the mixture of gases that surrounds Earth

equator—an imaginary line around the middle of Earth

evaporate—the action of a liquid changing into a gas; heat causes water to evaporate

pole—the top or bottom part of a planet

ray—a line of light that beams out from the sun

tilt—angle or leaning; not straight

Internet Sites

FactHound offers a safe, fun way to find Internet sites related to this book. All of the sites on FactHound have been researched by our staff.

Here's all you do:

Visit *www.facthound.com*

Type in this code: 9781620651667

Check out projects, games and lots more at
www.capstonekids.com

Glosario

la atmósfera—la mezcla de gases que rodea a la Tierra

el ecuador—una línea imaginaria alrededor de la mitad de la Tierra

evaporar—cuando un líquido se convierte en gas; el calor causa que el agua se evapore

inclinado—que está en ángulo o hacia un lado; no derecho

el polo—la parte superior o inferior de un planeta

el rayo—una línea de luz que sale del sol

Sitios de Internet

FactHound brinda una forma segura y divertida de encontrar sitios de Internet relacionados con este libro. Todos los sitios en FactHound han sido investigados por nuestro personal.

Esto es todo lo que tienes que hacer:

Visita *www.facthound.com*

Ingresa este código: 9781620651667

¡Algo súper divertido! Hay proyectos, juegos y mucho más en www.capstonekids.com

Index

Índice